This is a story about how I discovered a system for sourcing books in my pajamas.

-or-

"How I discovered the world's largest book source (Hint: It's Amazon)"

The embarrassing beginning

I began selling books on Amazon in 2007. After a prior entrepreneurial venture came to an end, I turned to bookselling after finding a $1 book at a garage sale which I resold for over $500.

My early days on Amazon were so humble, most of my early inventory came from a dumpster at the recycling center of a local university.

In those days, for an aspiring Amazon seller there were few resources to draw on. Only one guide to Amazon bookselling had been published, and there were no mentors or websites to turn to. Everything there   'ling on Amazon, I was teaching myself.

Fast forward to 2014

I had grown my business to six-figure sales working an average of 25 hours a week.

Then I moved to a new town two states away. Basically I wanted to live somewhere nicer and cooler (and more expensive) so I moved somewhere new where I only knew a couple people.

The move marked another shift, where I began to assess where this Amazon thing was going.

This was not a crisis of faith by any means. Rather, I began to look seriously at going to the next level by supplementing my existing business model.

I had to go in one of the two extremes:

- Scaling up and building a legit, large-volume bookselling operation.
- Or the other direction: adding some super automated passive revenue (like go-

ing the private label FBA route, which a lot of people are doing now).

Note I said "*supplementing* my existing business model." The scanning-every-thing-in-sight thing is in my blood. Reselling on Amazon is coded into my DNA at this point. That part wasn't going anywhere.

My dilemma: A lifestyle business vs. a business-business

On this existential quest, I had a bigger, identity-based question to answer.

There are two kinds of entrepreneurs (maybe three).

1.   Those who are fueled by the drive to build something. (The larger, the more satisfying.)
2.   Those who are led by lifestyle goals. (A specific level of freedom is sought, with a business created as the means).

A third, of course, is the person "just trying to make ends meet." Generally if you just want a small, comfortable living, you would just get a job and that "steady paycheck." But some may choose less volatile business pursuits to achieve the same thing.

I decided I was the second one. I was led by lifestyle. I like to travel, and do a thousand other things, and Amazon provides a perfect mobile business, allowing me to make my own hours (and get paid well for them).

So scaling up and building a large operation – with employees and infrastructure – might be in the cards for my future, but not yet.

So within the lifestyle-business framework, how do I scale up?

This is where we get into another one of my bookselling epiphanies. It's almost too simple, and it took me way too long to figure out.

It started with the "online arbitrage" trend that everyone was talking about.

For those that don't know, this is the practice of buying things online at one price, and reselling them elsewhere online at a higher price. It sounds so simple, and so appealing.

Which is why I hated any mention of "*online arbitrage.*"

Hated it. Rolled my eyes every time.

Basically, online arbitrage is fundamentally at odds with several of my beliefs about business, such as the "efficient market" hypothesis (basically that all significant price discrepancies are squeezed out of the market almost immediately), and how any "easy" business model becomes saturated almost immediately.

And everything I was hearing confirmed my suspicions

What I was hearing about online arbitrage indicated there was less opportunity than some of the hype would suggest.

That's not to say there aren't people making money, that's not to say there isn't sufficient opportunity to "buy low / sell high" online, and that's not to say there aren't people who are really good at it. But once a ton of people got on board with this idea, most of the "easy money" had been siphoned off.

At least that's what I was hearing.

And what I was hearing also indicated that what was left was a lot of opportunity if you were willing to sit on your inventory for awhile (like until Christmas), and accept lower margins than many are comfortable with.

But there was one "online arbitrage" idea I hadn't heard anyone talking about yet.

Most Amazon booksellers are part of what I call "cult of the $1 book." We're so spoiled with cheap inventory and high margins that we feel entitled to never pay more than $1 (or $2, depending on where you live) for anything.

This is why I always go for book sources that have high-priced books – most Amazon sellers won't touch them. I'm happy to pay $4, $5, or more for books if I know I'm going hit my desired profit margins. The secret is hedging your investment by knowing your numbers.

My epiphany in a dusty warehouse way out in the country

One day I was sourcing books at my most lucrative source - a large overstock store that received tons and tons of high-value books each week. With this particular source, there was one downside that set it apart from nearly every other source I frequented: The prices. For second-hand books, they were expensive. Each book was a flat $4 each.

Despite these prices, I was still able to earn a 300% return on my investment, and make easily over $1,000 a month off this one source. In fact, of the 50+ book sources I frequented, it was the single most lucrative.

One day it hit me: There was something special about that $4 number. It wasn't just the price of every book at my most lucrative source. It was the price of *the majority of used books on Amazon* (penny + $3.99 postage).

That was the lightbulb moment.

The best book source in the world might not be that overstock store. It might be Amazon itself.

What if it was possible to buy cheap books on Amazon, and resell at a much higher price via Fulfillment by Amazon (FBA)?

I decided to try it.

Testing this theory, I began to manually comb Amazon for cheap books that I could resell via Fulfillment by Amazon for a profit.

Although my manual methods were crude, they were working. At least a little.

Sales started to come in. Capitalizing on the huge pricing leverage offered by FBA, I was able to maintain my 300% margins paying $4 to $10 for books, and reselling at $20, $30, $40 and more. This insane idea was actually working.

I started to have the feeling of a guy who finds a bag of money on the street with a note attached that reads "Free Money." It felt too good to be true, or like some kind of trap. Was this against Amazon's rules? Why was no one doing this?

Still, it wasn't exactly the easiest job in the world...
On one hand, combing Amazon manually was kind of tedious. Due to the sheer volume of books on Amazon, and the relatively un-robust search options, the vast majority of the books I was looking at were duds.

On the other hand, I was finding enough that it was working out to about $30 an hour (*not making any income claims here - your results could deviate in either direction depending on how you apply this material*). Even if I found just a couple books an hour, it was pretty good for hanging out at Starbucks all day.

Even if I only found two books an hour using my primitive methods, if I was averaging a return of just $12 each, it wasn't bad for hanging out on the Starbucks patio.

And I could do it all day long.

And it was a source that never closed.

And it was a source that never got picked over.

Combined, I was beginning to think Amazon itself was the best book source anywhere.

Then I learned a couple tricks to using Amazon's search function, that increased the odds of finding profitable books. No "magic bullet" hacks, but things that increased my efficiency a little.

One example is the use of keywords. There were words that were extremely broad, and brought up a lot of extraneous results. And then I started to learn what keywords only applied to the kind of books I was looking for (mostly textbooks, because that was a niche I was familiar with.)

Then I discovered a few tools to streamline the process.

Eventually I contacted some mad scientist computer people who built me a tool to automate the process (that's not what this book is about, but I may share it with you in a future email).

I'd come a long way from my "book sourcing in my pajamas" fantasy, to making it a reality.

Before we get started...

You're probably wondering: If this tactic is so cool, why am I just giving it away to the world?

Well here's the bottom line: There are over 20 million books on Amazon. Thousands of niches. Nearly unlimited search variables. What are the chances we're finding the same books?

So with that said, here's to sourcing books in our pajamas...

-Peter Valley

(Short) Glossary

This isn't complicated, but if you're a newer seller there are a couple of terms you'll need to get acquainted with to understand this book.

FBA: Fulfillment by Amazon. Amazon's fulfillment service that allows us to price higher than other sellers, and makes all of this possible. Also known as "Prime eligible." (These terms are used interchangeably.)

MF (or merchant fulfilled): Any non-FBA offer from a third-party seller. Most offers on Amazon are merchant fulfilled (MF).

Prime: Amazon's subscription service that lets users get free shipping on all "Prime eligible" (aka FBA) offers. These are the primary customers we are targeting with online book arbitrage.

Sales rank (aka "best seller rank"): Amazon's measure of an item's demand. The better the sales rank (lower the number), the higher the demand and the more quickly we can expect the item to sell (and more boldly we can price). There's more to sales rank than this, so a cheat sheet has been added at the end of this book.

ONLINE BOOK ARBITRAGE

HOW TO SOURCE BOOKS ON AMAZON, & RESELL BACK ON AMAZON FOR A PROFIT

This book represents everything I know about how to source books from the Starbucks patio.

I'm not saying I was the first to do this, but I was the first to talk about it.

I started teaching the simple system I outline in this book in mid-2015. After I started making decent money with these methods, I announced a free webinar for readers of my website, FBAmastery.com.

Basically, I said "*Hey everyone, if you want to check out a system I developed for sourcing books online, I'm doing a webinar on Wednesday.*"

I never anticipated nearly 800 people would register. Apparently people were really hungry for this stuff.

And if you're reading this, you're probably hungry too.

Hungry people make the best learners, so let's get into it.

Before we get into the details, it's important to understand very specifically what online book arbitrage is about:

Purchasing cheap "merchant fulfilled" books on Amazon, and reselling at a much higher price with Fulfillment by Amazon.

Buy a book for $4, sell FBA for $35, and profit the difference.

Here's an example of a book I just found. This is what you can buy it for, used, right now:

Price + Shipping ≑	Condition (Learn more)	Delivery	Seller Information
$3.71 + $3.99 shipping + $0.00 estimated tax	**Used - Good** A copy that has been read, but remains in clean condition. All pa... » Read more	• **Arrives between** April 4-19. • Ships from TN, United States. • Domestic shipping rates and return policy.	goodwill_ind_of _mid_tn ☆☆☆☆☆ 96% positive over the past 12 months. (76,020 total ratings)

And here's what you can sell it for via FBA:

$29.99 *Prime* + $0.00 estimated tax	**Used - Very Good** No issues. Light bends in cover. Great book!	FULFILLMENT BY AMAZON ▾ • Free Two-Day Shipping: Get it Thursday, March 31 (order within 22hr 26min) • Domestic shipping rates and return policy.	Princeton Exchange ☆☆☆☆☆ 100% positive over the past 12 months. (2 total ratings)

After commissions, you will roughly triple your money. And there are thousands and thousands of offers like this all over Amazon, right now.

Everything we're going to talk about is built around this simple concept.

Make sense? Ok then, let's proceed...

Welcome to Online Book Arbitrage: About me

Let me quickly introduce myself. I'm Peter Valley.

I've been selling books on Amazon since 2007, and selling via FBA since early 2011.

Since the beginning of my Amazon journey, I've focused primarily on books. Currently books comprise 85% of my Amazon inventory.

I'm on my fifth year of six-figure sales.

I do a website called FBAmastery.com. I focus mostly on sourcing books and different tips and tricks to make more money on Amazon.

In addition to selling books, I've written a few such as "*Amazon Autopilot*" and "*Book Sourcing Secrets.*" I put out a bookselling DVD course, publish a bunch of free material I give away on FBAmastery.com, and lots more.

What you're going to learn

Let's get into what we're about to learn. I want you to know up front what value you're going to get from it so you know whether or not this book is going to be worth your time.

To start, I'm going to break down exactly why this works, so you understand the forces that underlie this system (and exactly why people will pay $50 for your book when they can get it for $10 from someone else).

I'm going to give you the four stages of book arbitrage's evolution as I have experienced it myself.

I'm going to teach you some tricks to help you find virtually endless books that you can buy low on Amazon and resell back on Amazon.

I'm going to share with you some tools that I discovered to streamline the online book arbitrage process.

I'm going to walk you through a real-time search on Amazon, and show you how I found books to resell for a profit in under 5 minutes.

And as a bonus, we're going to teach you a way to get all of your online sourced inventory for free. (I was literally conflicted on whether I wanted to reveal this tactic so publicly, but decided to at the last minute. I'll probably regret it later.)

And then we're going to cover every frequently asked question I've gotten since I started teaching this stuff last year.

Sound good?

So with that out of the way, these are the steps I went through from knowing nothing about online book arbitrage to making money...

My Journey Through Online Book Arbitrage

On my online book arbitrage journey, these are the four steps I went through:

The first phase was the **skepticism phase**. Basically, when I devised the theory that you could buy on Amazon and resell on Amazon, it seemed too good to be true. Even though I had been sourcing books in the second-hand market for years and applying a very similar pricing strategy (pricing my FBA offers much higher than regular offers, and waiting for sales), something about buying the books on *Amazon itself* seemed too easy (and too bold) to work.

So I began testing it. I started the way anyone would start, flailing around Amazon using broad searches, in a completely random fashion. This is where I got into what I call the **list-building phase**. I fumbled around Amazon and found a couple books here and there. And I started to notice patterns about books that you could buy low and resell high. And I started to take notes on certain titles and series of books that seemed to do well for book arbitrage. I kept track of those in an Excel file. That was my list-building phase.

The next phase was where I began to look more scientifically at the elements and factors that create arbitrage book value. What creates those giant price gaps? What are the exact factors of a book that has a big gap between the lowest merchant fulfilled (MF) price, and the lowest Prime-eligible (FBA) price? It is not random.

Books that can be flipped leave clues. So it's not just a matter of knowing what the FBA competition is and what the lowest merchant fulfilled offer is and just doing the math. There are more subtleties to it. This is what I call the **book arbitrage science phase**.

Then I got better, and I began to ask, "Okay, well, what tools can I use to streamline this process? Are there tools out there I can use to increase efficiency, instead of fumbling randomly around Amazon? This was **the streamlining phase**.

(We're going to get into what tools I discovered shortly.)

What makes this work?

Fundamentally all of this requires use of the pricing leverage offered by Fulfillment by Amazon. There are huge MF / FBA price gaps all over Amazon. If you already sell books on Amazon, you've seen this. Penny books can be selling for $35. Sometimes they'll have no FBA competition at all.

You see books all the time you can buy for a penny plus shipping and then you could sell those for $20, $25, sometimes $50 and up. That's fundamentally what we're talking about.

While we're going to talk a little bit about buying books on other sites and reselling on Amazon, really there is no competition. Amazon is the best source, hands down. It has the most books for the cheapest prices. I would say 90% of the time, Amazon has the cheapest copy of a book anywhere on the internet.

Why books are uniquely suited for online arbitrage

There are dozens of product categories on Amazon. Let me tell you why we're choosing books. Because this isn't random. It's important to understand why books are uniquely suitable for online arbitrage more than any other category I've studied.

Books are favorable for this reason: There are tons and tons and tons of cheap, used books on Amazon. More than any other category. There is more cheap, used stuff in the book category than any other.

This means there's lots of cheap merchant fulfilled copies of almost everything, waiting for us to buy them up and resell them FBA. The abundance of offers drives MF prices down. Huge opportunity for us.

Second, books are simply the biggest category on Amazon. There are some estimates as high as 40 million. (I think that number's a little inflated, and estimate it's more around like 20 million). Which makes Books the biggest category, and gives us virtually endless opportunity.

These are the two reasons that buying on Amazon and reselling on Amazon via FBA is definitely best done in the books category.

You're still in at the ground floor of this

Even though I've been teaching this method over the last year, it's been to relatively low numbers of Amazon sellers. So low, that I don't think the people doing this now are putting more than a small dent in the supply. Amazon is a big place.

To illustrate with hard numbers, the first "Online Book Arbitrage" webinar I gave saw close to 800 people register. About 550 logged in to attend. And how many of them do you think applied the material? While I got tons of glowing feedback, the sad fact is I expect that very few people went to work applying it.

There's a statistic that only 10% of books are read past the first chapter. And reading a book arguably takes less effort than effectively sourcing books online (note I said "effectively."). So the sad reality is that very few people are applying this formula right now. (Sad for the few, good for you).

This isn't easy: Good news disguised as bad news

I'm about to give you good news in disguise: The system I'm about to teach you is simple, but it's not easy. Amazon makes it extremely painful, actually. So for the few who actually figure out how this works and get good at it should have fertile fields available to them.

One of my fundamental business philosophies is that the harder something is, the more money there is to be made because fewer and fewer people are willing to persevere and master it.

So when I talk about how difficult Amazon makes these kinds of searches for us, consider that to be really good news in disguise.

Let's take a look at the only 3 things you need to understand to be a rock star at online book arbitrage.

Online book arbitrage fundamental #1: Why you can price much higher as an FBA seller.

If you're an experienced FBA bookseller, this part will be very familiar to you. If not, it's absolutely vital to understanding the rest of this book. Please read the next few paragraphs as many times as you need to for it to sink in and take root.

The practice of online book arbitrage is made possible by the incredible pricing leverage of Fulfillment by Amazon. FBA sellers can price offers into the stratosphere, and still get sales.

Example: A book selling for $1 + $3.99 postage, where the lowest FBA offer is $35. Assuming that book is in steady demand, someone will pay $35 to get that Prime-eligible offer.

FBA sellers can command prices literally 1000% higher (or more) than the lowest non-FBA offers.

Why? Because of the power of Amazon Prime.

$35.00 *Prime*
+ $0.00 estimated tax

Most FBA sellers know this already, but let's recap:

Number one, Prime subscribers want Prime eligible offers. They paid for their subscription, and will bypass lower-priced offers and pay more to get the free second day shipping, cheap overnight shipping, free tracking, guaranteed arrival dates, and liberal return policy. Often a lot more.

Number two, Prime offers (usually) get the "Buy Box." This is the biggest one. It's estimated *the majority of all sales* happen through the Buy Box.

The "Buy Box" as it appears for textbooks. Note the FBA offer displayed most prominently, despite many cheaper non-FBA offers.

Number three, urgency. Prime-eligible (FBA) offers appeal to those who need their books *now*. Any customer who is on a strict deadline (i.e. a student at the beginning of the semester) is likely to bypass all lower-priced offers and go directly for your premium-priced FBA offer.

The results bear out one huge fact: Amazon buyers will pay a lot more for FBA offers.

Online book arbitrage fundamental #2: How to price FBA offers.

Let's give an example: You have a book that's in high demand. The lowest used price is $5. Amazon is selling it for $50, and there's no FBA competition.

You can sell a book like this for $49. It doesn't matter if it's a textbook or anything else, a buyer will come along eventually.

You might sit on this a little longer than you otherwise would, but it will sell. Probably the single biggest mistake people make selling with FBA is they leave a ton of money on the table by failing to price boldly.

As an FBA seller, you are competing with other FBA sellers - no one else.

To succeed with this tactic, it's important to internalize this point. You must get over any mental barriers of doubt and just understand you *can* price things a lot higher with FBA and still get sales.

Once you understand that, the next step is to understand how to price textbooks. I'm going to talk a lot about textbooks in this book, but it is not necessary to focus solely on textbooks.

I was talking about this subject with somebody over email the other day and they said to me, "You focus too much on textbooks with online book arbitrage. You can really do this with anything." And I admit I'm a little biased. But I like textbooks because pricing rules go out the window.

To give a textbook-based example: Let's say there was a book that had not been ranked worse than a million over the last year (according to sales rank history, which we'll get into). Let's say there was no FBA competition. And let's say I could buy it for a penny + postage. In that case, I would list it at $50 right now. And I guarantee I'd get a sale, if not very quickly, at the beginning of the next school semester when sales surge.

Online book arbitrage fundamentals #3: Sales rank (aka "best seller rank")

Average Customer Review: ★★★★★ (52 customer reviews)
Amazon Best Sellers Rank: #200,136 in Books (See Top 100 in Books)

The next thing is to understand Amazon sales rank ("best seller rank"). I.e. what a rank of 700,000 means versus a rank of three million. This is going to be very central to doing online book arbitrage properly and understanding how book arbitrage works and making it effective for you.

I'm giving you a priceless cheat sheet on how to interpret sales rank at the end of this book. Use it.

Online book arbitrage fundamentals #4: How #1 through #3 interact

The next step is to understand how price, sales rank and other factors interact. None of these data points are of value in and of themselves. What's important is how they interact. Or to put it another way, what they mean in relation to each other.

For the purpose of online book arbitrage, a book that has a sales rank of two million but is selling for a penny is not the same as a book that's ranked 10,000 and selling for a penny. We're going to treat those books *very* differently.

Price is one thing. Sales rank is one thing. Together, they are *everything*.

Book arbitrage science: The seven factors that contribute to arbitrage value

What follows are the seven factors that make an arbitrage-able book (I just made up a word there. I freely admit that.)

Remember: *"Books that can be flipped leave clues."*

These are the seven clues.

To be successful, you must understand what these seven clues are.

Why are we talking about "looking for clues"? Why must we play Sherlock Holmes to find the FBA value of a book?

This is pretty simple (and mostly obvious): Amazon doesn't advertise the lowest FBA price in the search results. You have to click through to look at a book's product page, and then again to show FBA (aka "Prime eligible") offers. That takes a lot of time.

So if we didn't look at these "clues," here is what we would have to do:

1. Click a subject totally randomly.
2. Click on every book (again, randomly).
3. Click on the Prime button (or "Free Shipping") button to view FBA offers.
4. Repeat.

That's only three steps. But here's the thing: This kind of indiscriminate searching guarantees several calendar pages will blow away before you find your first $20 book. We don't have time for that.

It's so inefficient as to be pointless.

To illustrate how important the following seven clues are, let's take an extreme example: Let's say, for some bizarre reason, you were literally unable to see FBA offers. They were simply invisible.

Then let's say you were forced to make a living with online book arbitrage. But you can't even see the single piece of data that you need the most. It's invisible.

How would you know what books to buy?

What are the factors that contribute to the likelihood that a book can be bought low and sold high?

Although it sounds like some kind of Jedi skill, there is a way to get very close to knowing what books can be resold for a profit, without even seeing FBA offers.

That's what these seven factors are for.

Clue #1: The number of merchant-fulfilled offers.

hoices

This is perhaps the single most important.

There's a specific ratio that you can identify between the number of merchant-fulfilled offers and sales rank.

The lower that number, the higher the FBA prices.

The worse the sales rank the fewer number of merchant-fulfilled offers there can be before you can expect to find either no FBA offers, or high-priced FBA offers.

Conversely, the better the sales rank (lower the number), the more MF offers you can see and still expect to find either no FBA offers, or high-priced FBA offers.

The reason is very simple: There is a predictable ratio of FBA offers to merchant fulfilled offers at various sales ranks. When you know these ratios, you can "read between the lines,", and determine the likely volume of FBA competition.

I realize this seems kind of complex. But it's actually very simple.

You may have noticed by now, when I'm looking at a problem I like to analyze the data. And I undertook an extensive survey of Amazon offers to bring you the following table.

You do not need to memorize what follows. This table is just to illustrate how this works.

Note: Here I'm quoting an article I wrote on this subject. I mention "$7" because that is my threshold for offline sourcing. There is of course no money to be made in online book sourcing from buying books at $4 and reselling at $7. Ignore this figure and use this just to give you an idea of how this works.

If you're looking at the number of Used / New offers, and you see...

> **❝** More than 250 copies: These rarely have $7+ FBA offers. The peak percentage is 30%, for books ranked better than 5,000.
>
> 100 to 150 copies: Have $7+ offers over 50% of the time up to a sales rank of 10,000. Worse than that, the percentage drops dramatically.
>
> 50 to 100 copies: Have $7+ FBA offers 50% or more of the time up to a sales rank of 100,000.
>
> Fewer than 50 copies: Has $7+ FBA offers over 50% of the time up to a rank of 1 million (the worst rank studied). **❞**

Bottom line: The lower the number of copies for sale, the higher the chance there is high-priced FBA competition - or none at all.

This is a very important point.

Clue #2: Amazon's price.

$77.30 to buy ✓Prime

Amazon's price is always the ceiling. You can't out-price Amazon and expect to get a sale.

When we speak of "Amazon's price", we're referring to the price that Amazon sells if you buy it from them directly.

If that price is low, say if it's like $7 or $10, you cannot expect to make a profit from it with online book arbitrage. We need that price to be high. The higher the better.

Let's say you're purchasing a "penny book," i.e. a book selling for a penny + $3.99 postage. You will roughly start to double your $4 investment by selling that book for $14. That translates to roughly an $8 payout. There are many variables, but that's a rough rule of thumb.

So with this in mind, if we see a book selling for a penny, we need to see an Amazon price of at least $14.50 (because we still need to price a little below Amazon) to double our money. Make sense?

You can't outprice Amazon.

Now if Amazon is selling a book new from them directly for $50, that's even better news. We now have a much higher price ceiling. In the absence of other FBA competition, we can price that penny book all the way up to $49 (give or take) and still hope to get a sale.

Clue #3: Publication date.

This is by far the least important factor, but here's the guiding principle: The more recent the book the less likelihood you're going to find a glut of FBA offers and the more higher likelihood it'll be in demand.

This one is pretty obvious.

Clue #4: Price of the lowest used offer.

The higher the price of the cheapest copy, the higher the chance of high-priced FBA offers.

Everyone wants a deal, and there's no better deal than paying a penny (+postage) for a book you can flip for $35.

The Catch 22 is that penny books are the most likely to have a glut of FBA competition. There's still plenty of opportunity to be found in penny books, but the greatest opportunity is in books that cost more.

Starting with 2-cent books and going up, the opportunities become exponentially greater.

This fact gets even more pronounced when you get into the range of $10, $20 books. You will often find these have no FBA offers at all, and sky is the limit.

Now a lot of people don't have the stomach to invest that much in a single unit of inventory. So when you're online sourcing, you have to find out what your threshold is and only look for books that have a lowest price below that.

For the first several months I practiced online book arbitrage, I didn't spend more than $10 on a book. Since postage is $3.99, I was looking for books priced $6 or less.

There was still tons of opportunity at that level, but the opportunity opened up exponentially when I raised that limit. Today, I'll pay $25 for books and consistently sell them for $100 or more.

Part of the obstacle here isn't monetary, it's psychological. It's very uncomfortable for most people to invest $25 in a single unit of inventory.

The other psychological hurdle is believing a book can be sold for $75 more than the lowest MF price. If you've been selling books via FBA for a while I won't have to sell you on this point. But you will likely suffer some disbelief until you experience it.

You might not want to spend more than a penny for a book and there is still quite a bit of opportunity if you just wanted to spend a penny plus postage and resell those books for $18 or up. Not nearly as much than if you were willing to pay more, but still plenty of opportunity.

Clue #5: Type of book.

Textbooks are by far king here. There is seemingly no limit to how much more students will pay for Prime-eligible copies. Getting $25, $35, $50 (and more) above the lowest price is not uncommon.

On the other side, there are not many fiction titles you buy on Amazon and resell back on Amazon for a profit. That's why we're going to focus on non-fiction in this book. It's rare to find a fiction book with an Amazon price that is more than $15. Plenty of these exist, but unless they're recent releases, most of them have a glut of FBA copies.

On the other hand, textbooks can have Amazon prices that are literally $200, $250 and higher.

In between the two, are what we'll call "scholarly non-fiction." Not quite textbooks, but not mainstream non-fiction either. Tons and tons of arbitrage opportunity in this spectrum.

Clue #6: Sales rank.

The better the sales rank the faster that your high-price FBA offer will sell.

And the better the sales rank, the bolder you can be with your pricing and still get a sale.

This is why sales rank is so vitally important.

In the absence of other FBA competition, I wouldn't hesitate to take a book I bought for $4 and price at $100 if the rank was 5,000 (a really good rank).

Conversely, I wouldn't pay $4 for any book - no matter how low or non-existent the FBA competition - if it was ranked 2 million. Even 1 million is pushing it.

This is pretty obvious, but extremely important.

Clue #7: Sales rank *history*.

This is entirely different than sales rank.

Sales rank is just a snapshot in time. If it just sold a copy, a book ranked 150,000 could have been ranked 10 million 5 minutes ago, and not sold a copy in 5 years. A book ranked 150,000 could also be steadily selling one copy a day. All that sales rank tells us is what Amazon says its demand is *at that moment*.

Sales rank history is a much more accurate look at a book's demand. We can go back and look at a book's sales history over a 3 month, 6 month, and 12 month period to get more accurate info.

We'll get into exactly how to do that in a moment.

Isolating these factors through Amazon's search function

So now we know what data matters when searching for books that can be resold for a profit.

Now we're left with one HUGE question: Which of these can we search for on Amazon?

I have some good news and bad news here. Mostly bad, but enough good to keep you interested (I promise).

Amazon's search function was not designed with online book arbitrage in mind.

Shocking, I know. I'll give you a second to pick yourself up off the floor.

It's just a reality we have to work with.

It would all be so easy if we could take all seven of the key factors, run them through Amazon's search, and get a list of book arbitrage opportunities.

If we're going to find profitable books, Amazon is going to make us work for it.

So what can we search for?

Let's explore...

Examining Amazon's "Advanced search" page

Your Amazon searches have only one goal.

...and it is not to get Amazon to show you books you can resell for a profit.

Your goal is glass-half-empty:

The goal of your searches is to *eliminate the greatest number of unprofitable results.*

That's it.

We're not structuring our searches to find the best books. We're structuring them to eliminate the bad ones - as many as we can.

With that understanding, let's look at Amazon's "advanced search" function, and which of the seven "clues" can be searched for on Amazon.

Department ▾   S

Books   Advanced Search

Search option #1: Publication date.

Good news, Amazon lets us sort by publication date.

Bad news, because as I said, this is probably the least important data point.

Search option #2: Type of book.

Amazon lets us search by the type of book... sort of. We have two options here.

The category search: This is not very good. There's a lot of books that exist in multiple categories. But it lets us filter out some of the useless results.

For example, we can eliminate fiction books from our results. That's good.

Title search: We can (and should) also use the category search in conjunction with keywords using the "Title" keyword search field. That's even better.

So these options do help, and when used together are the best options we have.

Search option #3: Sales rank.

Ostensibly, Amazon gives us the option to sort by sales rank (the option is called "best selling").

Any reasonable person using the "best selling" option would expect you would get every result you're searching for, from best ranked to worst. What else could it possibly mean, right?

In practice, it doesn't do that. It only does that "sort of" (get used to those two words, they come up a lot in this chapter).

Reality is, Amazon spits out the results in a seemingly random order. They're roughly in order from bestselling to least, but a huge majority of results seem to be excluded. Why? No one knows.

What's provable is that if you search by "best selling" in Amazon's advanced search function, Amazon does not search for every single book with the title key word that you gave it in exactly the order of best sales rank to worst sales rank. It *tells* you that's what it's doing. But it's not doing that.

Search option #4: Price of lowest offer.

Just like with sales rank, Amazon tells us it will sort by the price of the lowest offer. In practice, it barely does this. Again, it seemingly spits out results in a random order.

Sometimes it will show you the penny books in some random order, not sorted by sales rank. And sometimes it will sort lowest to highest based on the price to buy it from Amazon directly. It's very weird, and very arbitrary.

I have a couple of theories as to how its algorithm works. I think what it's doing is only showing books that have a strong sales history and leaves out the rest. Just type in "biology" and there will be tons of things that it does not show you. Why? Only the people who code Amazon's algorithms know.

Amazon's search options: A recap

You're probably saying, "Well, we can search for four out of seven 'clues', and that isn't bad. Right?"

First, it's not four out of seven. It's more like 2.5 out of seven.

But here's the biggest problem: It's not about how each of these factors exist in isolation, it's how they *interact*.

As covered, Amazon really only lets us search for two or maybe two-and-a-half of those at the same time. And even those are pretty weak.

None of this should be taken as discouraging. As we'll see in a second, there's still plenty we can do with the options we have.

These search options allow us to get a little closer to profitable results, and eliminate a lot of the extraneous results. It gives a little more focus to our search results, and that's a lot better than nothing.

Let's indulge in a brief book arbitrage fantasy...

Let's say you could do a search for books ranked better than 100,000 that have a publication date of 2010 or more recent and are textbooks and have less than 30 used offers.

If you could do that, that would be simply amazing. It would be like printing money.

You'd be able to hone in very, very specifically on books that you could resell for a profit.

If we wanted to find and just really cut out all the extraneous search results and just really hone in on exactly the books that would have the highest likelihood of being able to be resold for a profit, the search function would allow us to do searches like that.

Or to take this fantasy further, it would be having a magic button where you could just say, "Show me all the books ranked better than 100,000 with no FBA offers at all." That's probably never going to happen (but it would be awesome).

Let's get into this a little more. What *specifically* would a dream Amazon search look like if we could sort of redesign Amazon's advanced search options?

The search factors we wish we had (but don't)

- An option to limit the number of used offers so we can increase the chances of there being no FBA competition (or really high-price FBA competition).

- An option to sort by sales rank (one that actually worked).

- An option to sort by keyword.

- And an option to sort by lowest used price to highest used price.

- And an option to search within a price range, such as books selling used for no less than, say, $0.02 and no more than $5.00.

If we could have a dream search it would probably look something like that.

Remember the only goal with online book arbitrage searches

It's important to remember this when you're figuring out how to structure your searches.

The goal is *not* to get Amazon to show you just the books that you can resell for a profit. That search option doesn't exist and it probably never will.

The goal of your searching is to *eliminate the greatest number of extraneous results.*

That's it. We're trying to cut out as much noise as possible.

That is going be accomplished through the combination of using the couple of search options that actually work, and well-chosen search words.

Before we do a search, we have to lay some groundwork...

Laying the groundwork for profitable searches

1. Decide exactly what you can pay.

Set a maximum amount per unit that you're willing to invest. Keep in mind that you're going to pay $3.99 for shipping. So know what number you need to see and ignore anything over that. Have a hard line in the sand that you won't breach.

This is important because we're trying to streamline the search process, and having firm rules will eliminate hundreds of small decisions as you search.

2. Establish your goal.

Let's say you want to do textbooks. That's what I tend to focus on. So we're looking for terms that will only exist in the titles of textbooks.

You can't just type in "textbook" and return every textbook. Not only can you not do that, you shouldn't want to. There are hundreds of thousands of textbooks. That's too broad.

To do this properly we want to strike a balance between too obscure and too common. You'll be entering this keyword into the "title" search field in Amazon's "advanced search."

Example:

> Too common: Biology (286,869 results)

> Too obscure: Dendrology (146 results)

If I had to choose, I would go with dendrology before biology, but we can usually get results that are somewhere in between.

Why don't I just give you a long list of profitable keywords here? Be glad I'm not. There are lots of people reading this book. And everyone would be doing the same searches.

It's not hard to do a little Googling and pull up glossaries for various fields of study. Within those glossaries, you can find countless specialized search terms. And there are thousands and thousands of niches to choose from. You won't be victim to a shortage of options here unless you suffer from a shortage of creativity.

Searching for books on Amazon

Where the rubber meets the road:
A step-by-step guide

So we just got a lot closer to eliminating all the extraneous stuff - the Harry Potters and romance novels and such. This is a big step towards finding profitable books.

Now that we understand all of this, we're at the fun part: Searching for books. **Step #1: Head over to Amazon's "advanced search" page.**

You have to first go to the Book category. At the top (but below the search bar) on the left side, you will see the words "advanced search." Click that.

Step #2: Set your title keyword.

Remember we're going for the right balance between too broad and too narrow. Enter your chosen word or phrase in the "Title" field.

Step #3: Set publication date

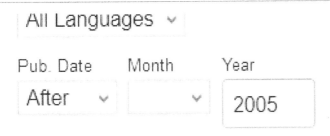

Since we decided on looking for textbooks, publication date is going to be even more important. It's hard to find really old textbooks that are still in demand, right?

On the flip side, most people think that no one is buying textbooks unless they're the most recent edition(s). That's totally wrong.

I would say when you get older than 2005 it starts to get dramatically less likely that people are still buying that textbook. The key is here is to always defer to the sales rank history. That's the only way in which demand is measured. We'll go into that in a moment.

Set the search date parameters at after 2005. We just eliminated all the older textbooks that will never sell.

We're getting closer.

Step #4: Set subject category

Amazon does not have a category for "textbooks."

But when we choose our search word (or search term), we can pretty accurately surmise what category the books we're looking for will be in.

For example, let's say we were going with "dendrology" (even though I recommend against it). We can assume the books we're looking for are under "Science and Math." Select that.

Again, we're trying to eliminate more useless results. (Though, realistically, the word "dendrology" is so scientific its unlikely to show up in any children's or romance book titles).

More bad results eliminated. Getting closer.

Step #5: Set the format.

Format

All Formats ⌄

This is an important one.

This isn't about picking a format that will bring up the most profitable results. All we're trying to do here is *eliminate* Kindle books from the results. We don't care about Kindle.

So pick either paperback or hardback. It doesn't matter.

We just eliminated even more useless results. We're getting even closer.

(Optional) Step #5.5: Sort by "best selling."

This is optional because it is best applied only when your keywords bring up a relatively small number of results.

How small is "small"? There's no hard math to rely on here, but if you hit search and you see less than 30,000 results, I would consider sorting by "best selling".

Amazon seems to favor better-ranked books whether you use this or not, but it does even more so when you tell it to. And since the majority of results are always going to be laden with low-demand books, this can help with that.

The reason we don't use this with broader searches is that Amazon will favor books that cost more, and the first many pages are likely to be laden with expensive books.

However, if you are in the strata of seller who is willing to invest $15+ per book, then 1) My hat is off to you. You'll do well with online book arbitrage, and 2) You should ignore this and *always* sort by best-selling.

Step #6: Hit search.

Search

(Optional) Step #6.5. Skip ahead several pages.

If you're sorting by best selling, skip ahead at least 3 pages. The first few pages of results are unlikely to have low-priced used offers.

Step #7: Start going through the results.

Start visually scanning the results. We're reviewing the listings looking for low-priced used offers that are within our price range. I'm no longer afraid to spend serious money on a book. Many might not be willing to pay more than $1 and that's totally fine. There's lots of opportunity either way.

It's important at this stage to keep in mind everything we've talked about up to this point. Because we're going to rely on what we can see in the search results to decide which items to click on and investigate more closely.

Remember we cannot see crucial data like sales rank and lowest FBA offer in the search results. To see that, we have to click over and view the product page. We're trying to avoid doing that with anything that doesn't have a high likelihood of being profitable.

This is where the seven "clues" I talked about come in. We're going to start looking for more of those.

As we're visually scanning the search results, we are looking for these things:

A high Amazon price. This is the number with the Prime logo next to it. Amazon won't show the Prime value for third-party offers, just books they are selling directly (which is always higher than we'll be able to sell it for).

For example, if you're aiming for a minimum of doubling your money, look for an Amazon price that's at least $15. And only then if the cheapest used price is a penny. (Remember the rough payout for a $14 book when sold FBA is about $8, or double the cost of that penny book).

Next, we're looking for...

Books in your price range. Remember when I told you to have a firm price ceiling and not go over it? That was to make this part go very quick.

Let's say you're not willing to pay more than $10 per book. You're going to look for any book for which the lowest copy is $6 or under (or, I guess, $6.01 or under if you want to get exact).

Next up, we're looking for...

A low number of offers for sale. Either new or used, look for books with less than 125 offers. This shouldn't be a hard rule, because there is opportunity above that with high-demand books, but keeping it under 125 is a good rule of thumb.

You should be able to assess all three of these in a split second.

When everything checks out, we're going to click on a book and investigate further...

Step #8: Start clicking.

Remember: High Amazon price, lowest price under your threshold, total number of offers is under 125.

When all of those apply, click on "used and new."

This brings us to all the book's available offers. But we're not looking at prices yet. First we're going to...

Step #9: Look at the sales rank and sales rank history.

We can do both in one swoop.

To do this, I'm going to ask you to install a browser extension called Keepa. If you're an experienced Amazon seller, you may have this installed already.

This embeds Amazon sales rank data directly on the Amazon product page. When you click "used and new," you'll see the Keepa data just below the product image.

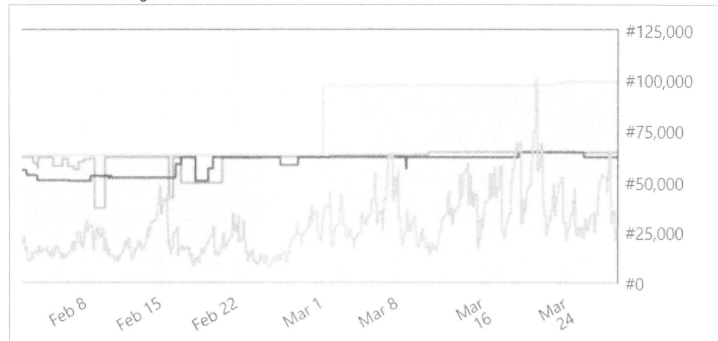

The data is displayed in graph form, and you'll be given the option to view sales rank data for that day, week, month, 3 months, year, or all time.

Take a look at what the rank is right now, and what the *worst* rank has been in the last 3 months.

Personally, I get nervous when I see something has been worse than 1 million in the last 3 months. But I will go as high as 1.2 million when I'm in the mood.

I know people who are considerably more liberal than myself, and will go all the way to 2 million and beyond. This can work, but keep in mind you'll sit on your books longer.

(What do all these sales rank numbers actually mean? I included a cheat sheet at the end of the book. Worth its weight in gold.)

Step #10: Click to view FBA offers only.

If everything checks out, now we're going to view the "Prime eligible" (aka FBA) offers. This is where we learn what we can sell it for (or give us a starting point).

Refine by Clear all

Shipping

☐ ✓*Prime*

☐ Free shipping

Just click on the "Prime" option in the right hand column (if you don't subscribe to Prime, or aren't signed in, click "free shipping.")

That will bring up the FBA offers only, from lowest to highest.

So what exactly are we looking for?

The majority of the time, we will plan to match the lowest FBA price. Let's say the lowest merchant fulfilled copy is $1 + $3.99 postage ($4.99 total).

Then let's also assume we're aiming to triple our money. ($15 payout).

To get a $15 payout, we need to aim to sell the book for roughly $22.50 or more. So if the cheapest FBA offer for this book is less than that, we should move on to the search results and keep looking.

But keep in mind most people are very happy to merely double their money (especially if they don't have to get out of bed to do it).

In that case, we only need to sell our book for $16.75 (or less if the book is lighter). That equates to roughly a $10 payout.

Then consider 50% profit margins are considered good in most businesses.

In that case, we only need to sell the book for $12. With a larger book, that equates to roughly a $6 payout.

There is a common scenario we want to keep in mind: Quite often, we'll want to *ignore* the lowest FBA offer, and plan to price above it. Perhaps we want to match the second-lowest FBA offer (or just price somewhere in between).

The subject of Amazon pricing strategy is way outside the scope of this book, but once again the general rule is: The greater the demand for a book, the bolder we can be with our pricing.

With high-demand books, we don't have to be the lowest FBA price. We can be second or third, and have confidence the cheaper copies will sell out, and we'll be next in line.

This is a very important point, and an exponentially greater amount of options open up if you're willing to price above the lowest FBA offer, hold your ground, and wait for a sale.

I'm including a profit margin cheat sheet at the end of this book to use as reference.

Sound good? Let's move on...

(Optional) Step #10.5: Look for cheaper copies on other sites

I would estimate that 90% of the time, Amazon is going to have the cheapest copy of a book anywhere on the internet.

It's extremely rare to find a book that's selling for say $5 on Amazon that's selling for $0.50 on another site. But it's not too uncommon to find books that are a dollar or two less on other sites.

To do this kind of comparison shopping, I'm going to ask you to install two browser plug-ins:

- Context Search (https://addons.mozilla.org/en-US/firefox/addon/context-search/)
- AddAll (http://www.addall.com)

The function of Context Search is it lets you highlight any text, then right-click and run the highlighted text through one of various search engines or websites.

We're going to use that in conjunction with AddAll - a book price comparison site.

Store	Book Price	Shipping Charge	Sales Tax	Total Cost in USD	Order Processing Time	Shipping Time	Click to Buy
Amazon.co.uk *UK* (*MARKETPLACE-USED*)	35.50	9.85	0	45.35	Available	Airmail / 7-21 days	Buy
Amazon.co.uk *UK* (*MARKETPLACE-USED*)	35.50	9.85	0	45.35	Available	Standard / 7-12 days	Buy
Alibris (*NEW/USED*)	50.05	0	0	**50.05**	See Site	USPS / 3-14 days	Buy

When you install both of those, you will be able to highlight the ISBN of a book (in the item description on every book's product page), then right click, choose "AddAll," and run that ISBN through over a dozen sites.

Often, you will find a cheaper copy and boost your margins.

Step #11: Buy the book

You've done it

You've found a reasonably well-ranked book with a big gap between the price you're going to pay, and the FBA price you can sell it for.

All that's left is to buy the book, ship it into Amazon, and profit the difference.

Pretty cool that we live in a time when we can literally turn a profit from our love seat while watching TV. *What a time to be alive...*

A real time online book arbitrage search

Putting all of this into action

Putting this into action: Doing a live search

So let's get into a real-time example.

To put my money where my mouth is, I'm going to walk you through a real search (as in, I'm actually going to do a search and record the results) to show you how this is done.

(As a bonus, I recorded this search so you can see it in action. I'll send you a link to the recording over email. If you don't get it soon, email me at fbamastery@gmail.com)

Let's begin

I've decided I'm going to find a textbook, and I'm going to keep my cost to $10 and under, and I want to at minimum double my money.

So with those parameters set, I'm first going to Amazon's advanced search page.

Next I put my cursor in the title keyword search, and have to ask myself: What's a textbook title search term that's not too broad, but not too narrow? I'll go with "*Immunology*." Not too broad, not too narrow.

(Disclaimer: It's probably a mistake to attempt this search after this book comes out. Hundreds or thousands of people dog piling on "immunology" is bound to result in opportunity here being siphoned off.)

I'll select "Paperback" to weed out the Kindle results. I could have just as easily chosen "Hardcover", it doesn't matter.

I'll then sort by the "Medicine" category.

And then I'll sort by best-selling. "Immunology" is bringing up around 18,000 results in paperbacks. This is under the 30,000 suggested threshold, so I'm going to sort by best selling.

Then I hit search.

I'll always glance at the first page, but when I use the "sort by best-selling" option, I usually want to skip ahead a few pages. As usual, the first few pages appear to have really high-priced books that are outside my price range.

So I check out one book on the first page. It's the lowest-priced book, and was selling for $7, outside my range.

The first book that looks like it has potential is three pages in: *"Immunology: A Short Course"*.

The lowest priced copy is selling for a penny. Well under $10. So far so good.

So I'll click over and first look at Keepa, and the sales rank history. This book has not been ranked worse than 500,000 for at least the last three months. A very strong demand.

Next I'll sort by Prime offers, to see what we can sell this for.

The lowest Amazon offer is $22.78 - and that's an Acceptable condition offer. We can often price higher than Acceptable offers, because a lot of buyers pass on those.

This is a great book.

Because at the time I'm typing this we are just before "textbook season" (the beginning of each semester when textbook sales surge), I plan to skip the two lowest offers, and price this at $35.00.

That translates to roughly a $26 payout, or more than 6 times my investment. A big winner.

But I'm not done.

I want to see if I can find another winner with "immunology."

I keep skimming the results, looking for more offers that fit my criteria.

I see another book that looks hopeful, simply titled *"Immunology For Medical Students."*

It is also selling for a penny. So far so good.

According to Keepa, it has not been ranked worse than 800,000 in the last three months. Very respectable rank. This is looking promising.

I click to view Prime offers. The lowest copy is selling for $21.39. Given the time of year, I would skip that one. With no other FBA offers, I will probably price this at $45. Maybe more.

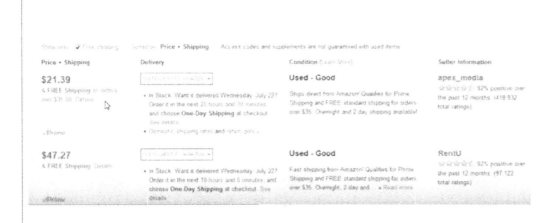

I'll quit while I'm ahead.

So for less than 5 minutes work, I found two books, spent $8, and expect to profit over $50.

It really is that simple.

Reviewing the live search

This is at once very simple and very not simple.

It's hard because it's kind of difficult to create a system out of this.

But it is easy because you're just hanging out on the internet in your pajamas making money.

So in our real-time example, we searched for "immunology," then we found a couple books with big price gaps. We can buy them each for a penny and resell for $35, $45, maybe more.

So let's recap what we just did.

1. We picked the maximum amount we're willing to spend,
2. We picked a narrow search term.
3. We went into Amazon's advanced search, and entered a title keyword.

4. We sorted by best selling (contingent).

5. We visually scanned the first results that come up.

6. We inspected for a high Amazon cover price, and total number of copies under 125.

7. We checked sales rank history through the Keepa extension.

8. We checked for the lowest FBA offer.

9. We checked prices on other sites (optional).

10. We bought the book.

Pretty simple.

You can make a lot of money following exactly these steps.

Advanced tricks

Search hacks
Search tricks
More tools
Calculating net profits
Top 7 ways to make money
Super-advanced tricks
Amazon gift card arbitrage
How to avoid the only two mistakes you can make

Search hack: Using negative keywords

Here's a cool and useful search-hack I haven't talked about yet: Using negative keywords.

Remember the point I made repeatedly about the goal of your searches being to eliminate the greatest number of unprofitable results? This further helps accomplish that, very efficiently.

How it's done: You place a minus ("-") sign before any word in the search bar, and this will filter out any results that have that word in the title.

For example, let's say you do a search, and its returning tons of Cliffs Notes. We don't do business in Cliffs Notes, because Amazon is selling all of them directly for under $7.

You can just type minus ("-") and the word "Cliffs" and that will eliminate those results.

Pretty cool.

Advanced search tricks

Searching for previous editions: Let's say you see a book that is just outside your price range. For example, a book that looks great, except it's $6.50 and you're not willing to pay more than $5.00.

If it's the 7th edition go ahead and search for the 6th edition. You will often find there's still a very strong demand for that book but it's going to be a lot cheaper almost all the time.

Look at the number of reviews when you're visually scanning. Don't emphasize this one too much, but a book with no (or very few) reviews is probably a book that isn't selling very often. This can help further streamline the search.

Focus on a single publisher. Another cool trick. If you know a publisher that publishes the kinds of books that you want to resell, Amazon has an option in the advanced search to search just for a particular publisher.

This might be something you don't start to use until you get a feel for who publishes the kind of books you're looking for, but it can be very useful.

If you're doing textbooks keep it to the last 10 years. I touched on this earlier, but this is a good rule of thumb. There are plenty of older textbooks still selling, but this is a good rule of thumb. It helps limit some of the noise.

Streamlining the process: Tools for online book arbitrage

Let's recap the tools I've mentioned so far, and talk about two I haven't.

Book Burro: This Firefox browser extension compares the book you're looking at (which it automatically detects) across several other bookselling sites (including Half.com and Powells). Its not as extensive as AddAll (which we talked about earlier), but the benefit is that you don't have to leave the page to use it. Everything appears in simple drop-down form in the corner of the page.

How Many? extention: This cool browser extension solves a common book arbitrage problem I haven't even talked about yet: Competing sellers who have multiple copies of the same book.

Let's say you're thinking about buying a copy of "*Immunology 101.*" It's selling for $1 merchant fulfilled. But there is one lowball FBA offer of $6.99 from megaseller "RentU." The rank is good, so you're tempted price your copy above it, at $25.

But there's one problem: Often times, megasellers can have dozens of copies of each book. You might not be waiting for one copy to sell out, you might be waiting for 50. How do you know exactly how many copies of this book the lowball seller has for sale?

This extension gives the answer by displaying the number of units in stock for each item just below the price. Very cool!

It's not free, but it's cheap. Check it out at:

https://chrome.google.com/webstore/detail/how-many/fifaampimdjablpkjapdjehjcfloecjp

And the two extensions we covered already:

• Keepa
• Context Search + AddAll

Both are must-have's.

Calculating your net profits

If you're new to FBA, you might not have a good feel for Amazon's commissions. You might see a book you can sell for $35, but you're not quite sure what that translates to in terms of your actual payout.

Until you get a feel for it, you can use the FBA Revenue Calculator.

https://sellercentral.amazon.com/hz/fba/profitabilitycalculator/index?lang=en_US

This is a simple tool offered by Amazon that lets you enter an ISBN, enter a price, and it will tell you what your payout will be after all the various fees and commissions are taken out.

You'll quickly get a feel for these numbers and have them memorized, but when you're getting started it can help to keep the FBA calculator tab open while you're doing your searches.

There is also a Firefox and Chrome extension that does essentially the same thing.

Chrome:
https://chrome.google.com/webstore/detail/amazon-fba-calculator-aut/hiboi pckpnehmbhkpkblbcenpfdekdhf?hl=en-US

Firefox:
https://addons.mozilla.org/EN-us/firefox/addon/fba-calculator-widget/

The top 7 ways to make money with online book arbitrage

#1: Be willing to pay more than a penny

Everyone wants a deal, and there's no better deal than paying a penny (+postage) for a book you can flip for $35.

The Catch 22 is that penny books are the most likely to have a glut of FBA competition. There's still plenty of opportunity to be found in penny books, but the greatest opportunity is in books that cost more.

Starting with 2-cent books and going up, the opportunities become exponentially greater.

And when you get into $15+ territory, you pretty much own the internet.

#2: Know how to find textbooks

Without question, some of the best opportunity is in textbooks. I don't recommend you limit yourself to textbooks, but it's a profitable place to start.

Understand the common characteristics of textbooks (high Amazon price / cover price, title keywords), use them in the search options, and then visually scan book titles in the results to identify textbooks.

#3: Use keyword title searches

Many sellers have a particular niche of book they know to be profitable. Others have a list of particular titles they search for daily or weekly. Use the title keyword option to find the specific book (or type of book) you're looking for.

#4: Don't go for the most well-ranked books

It's very tempting to focus your searches on the best-ranked items that will sell fast. And this is a smart strategy. Yet when you do sales rank-based purchases, keep a few things in mind: A sales rank you think is "bad," might not be that bad.

There is a lot of misconception among sellers about what constitutes a "good" sales rank and a "bad" sales rank. Many sellers naively believe anything ranked worse than 500,000 is a "poor selling" title.

Refer to the "sales rank cheat sheet" at the end of this book for the real story.

#5: Doing textbooks? Consider what time of year it is.

Even textbooks ranked 1 million (or worse) in the "off season" can hold a rank of better than 200,000 for a solid month during the fall and winter textbook season. Don't be mistaken: Textbooks will sell *all year round*, however sales will spike during certain times of year (the only noticeable "valleys" are in the middle of each semester, and the end of each semester).

When you understand this, you have a huge advantage over other sellers who shy away from books with a less-than-good sales rank during the off-season.

#6: Accept lower margins

Everyone wants the well-ranked book they can flip for 500% profits. And such opportunities are common, but they're not limitless.

But there is an abundance of offers you can resell for double your money.

And there is a virtually limitless supply of offers you can get 50%+ returns on.

When you consider most businesses operate with a profit margin of 40% or less, you are in the privileged position of having a business in which you can double your money all day long, without even leaving your computer.

#7: Don't be deterred by the presence of low-ball FBA offers

You will encounter many, many products with a low-ball FBA offer that doesn't allow for your desired profit margin. But you don't always have to compete with the lowest FBA offer. You can be the 2nd or 3rd lowest, and when the low-ball offers sell out, you'll be the next sale.

The better the sales rank (and sales rank history, as revealed via Keepa), the less you should be deterred.

Advanced online book arbitrage tactics

So here's some next-level stuff, the last of which I really hesitated about sharing publicly.

Set up price alerts with Keepa. If you see a book that's just outside your price range, you can set up a price alert with Keepa. You're basically saying

"I'm not willing to pay \$6.50 for this, but I am willing to pay \$5" and Keepa will alert you immediately when the price drops to \$5.

Outsource everything. There are companies who, for a fee, will allow you to ship your books to them, and they will then prepare your books and ship them to Amazon for you. And they'll do this for as little as \$1 per book.

You're reading this right: You can literally run a bookselling operation without even touching a book.

Here's the catch: Right now, there simply aren't many of these companies who will work with you.

The reason is that FBA users are surging, and many such companies are at capacity and aren't accepting new clients. Many others have very high minimums that are prohibitive for online arbitrage. And many simply won't accept books. (With this type of service, it's a seller's market all around).

I've contacted nearly all of the companies out there, and I found only *one single company* that is a good fit for practitioners of online book arbitrage.

Because (as of the time of this writing) there aren't enough companies like this to go around, I'm only sharing the name of this company on a one-on-one basis, so they don't get overwhelmed.

To filter out the tire-kickers, I'll share the name of this company (with which I have no affiliation and receive no compensation) if you email me personally at fbamastery@gmail.com.

International arbitrage. The AddAll extension I talked about shows Amazon prices on many international sites. It's not terribly common, but you will see books that are selling for \$100 in the US that you can get for, say, \$15 overseas. You'll pay a lot for postage but you can still make money.

Do you remember a book by an author called Neil Strauss called "*The Game*"? It came out in 2007 or so. It was a big seller and it mentioned another book called "*Introducing NLP.*" I think the author of "*Introducing NLP*" did not anticipate a mere mention creating a huge surge in demand for his obscure book, and probably didn't even know it was mentioned in a bestseller until his book sold out across the US.

At the time it was a big hit here, *The Game* apparently hadn't caught on in the UK. You could still find copies of *Introducing NLP* there. I went on Amazon.co.uk and I literally bought 15 copies at $15 and turned around and resold them for over $100 each on Amazon.com.

Ebay arbitrage. There are two ways to source on Ebay.

One is to find cheaper copies on Ebay than you can find on Amazon, and then resell them via Fulfillment by Amazon. You can set up alerts, where eBay will email you when a book shows up within a price range that you set. Very cool.

A second method is to buy wholesale lots of books on eBay, break them up, and resell on Amazon. Takes a little work and a keen eye for value, but often profitable.

Amazon gift card arbitrage

This was my personal secret for a long time. I'm probably going to put myself out of business here by talking about this publicly, but I want to thank you for reading this far. So have fun with this one.

Textbook gift arbitrage goes like this:

1. Go to the Amazon textbook buy-back page.

http://www.amazon.com/Sell-Books/b?node=2205237011

2. Type a keyword in the search bar to narrow the results a little, just as you would with "normal" online book arbitrage.

It will bring up a list of books that Amazon is willing to give us Amazon store credit for. There's two really cool things about this:

One, the amount you see is guaranteed if you get that book to Amazon any time in the next two weeks.

Two, Amazon pays for the shipping. So you don't have to do any crazy math here.

The only trick is finding cheaper used copies anywhere in the vast terrain of the internet. If you can find any copy of that book anywhere, for lower amount, you get to pocket the difference.

3. So now we start using the Context Search / AddAll trick, and combing the internet for cheaper copies.

Is there a light bulb going off now?

Then we can use the trade credit to fund our online book arbitrage (or buy lots of junk food, or get our girlfriends something, or whatever).

The trick here is that it's very different than the type of online book arbitrage we've talked about up to this point in one key way: You have to spend $120 to make $30. So the margins are much lower.

For that reason, I'm generally looking for books with a trade-in value of over $100. That's where I find the most opportunity.

You can't expect to triple your money or even double your money or even make 50% returns with Amazon gift card arbitrage. You have to be willing to spend a lot of money to make 10% or 20%. But it adds up.

Losing money is not a concern, because this number is locked in. You know you're making money when you buy. There's no chance the price will drop, or a lowball seller will come in and underprice you, or all the usual concerns with online book arbitrage.

So I won't even care if I'm spending $100 and only making $10. That $10 is guaranteed, and it amounts to just a few minutes of work.

This is where those tools I talked about earlier become even more useful - Book Burro, and the AddAll / Context Search combo.

All you need to do is find a single copy anywhere on the internet less than that trade-in amount, and you get to keep the difference. Very cool.

How not to screw up online book arbitrage

There are only two major ways you can lose money with online book arbitrage.

1. Ignoring sales rank history
Amazon sales rank doesn't tell the whole story. If its a good rank, all that tells you is that the book sold recently - not when it will sell again.

The real story is told in its sales rank history. Which is why I recommend using Keepa to view historical data and get a sense of the book's overall average rank - not just what it is today.

Ignore this data, and risk purchasing a book that has only enjoyed a temporary spike in sales, vs. a consistently in-demand title.

2. Not keeping your prices competitive
You should be repricing your books regularly to keep them "competitive."

But what does "competitive" mean?

One thing it *doesn't* necessarily mean is always keeping your FBA offers the lowest price. It also doesn't necessarily mean keeping your offers matching the lowest price. Much (if not most) of the time, you'll find it's more strategic to price higher, and wait for lowball offers to sell out.

Whatever your pricing strategy, you'll want to regularly look at your prices. Often this will mean raising them. Other times, you will find you've been undercut by other sellers, and will want to drop your prices.

But keep an eye on those prices.

Conclusion

You can do exactly what I just showed you in this book and make a bunch of money right now.

If you only put in a few hours a day, you found two books an hour, and you only worked five days a week that's just about an extra $1,000 dollars a month with the system we just outlined.

And you can do it from a hot tub (no splashing).

Live Q&A on online book arbitrage

Live audience questions from my private online book arbitrage group, more.

Live Online Event

Online Book Arbitrage

Presenter
Peter Valley

"How to find books on Amazon to resell on Amazon."

With Peter Valley

The Q&A that follows comes from two sources:

1. The first "Online Book Arbitrage" webinar.
2. My super-secret online book arbitrage group calls that happen once or twice a month. (I don't talk about this much, but if you want to be on these calls send me an email: fbamastery@gmail.com)

These were recorded live. Some of the questions and answers have been edited for clarity.

Q: "Why would an FBA buyer pay $25 for something that they could buy for $4?"

That is the biggest question of all. I'm so glad you asked that. And honestly, I'm at risk here of sounding kind of flippant as I've said multiple times. But if you don't understand that basic concept, seriously, [online book arbitrage] might not be the best for you because what's fundamental to carrying this out is being able to price boldly.

One of the reasons is a total mystery. Why people pay that much. I would never pay that much. But the fact is that it works and that's all that matters.

That's my short answer. The large answer or the longer answer is FBA and Prime Eligible offers offer huge, huge, huge advantages particularly for people that want books immediately and they get that free second-day shipping. A lot of people are willing to pay astronomical amounts more for FBA offers. More than they would merchant-fulfilled. And it doesn't so much matter if you wouldn't. It just matters that it works.

Anyone who's an FBA seller can jump in and testify that you can find a penny book that's ranked 100,000 and if there's no FBA competition and Amazon's selling it for $100 you could price that book for $50 and get the sale.

Q: "Are you allowed to use your Prime account to buy books?"

I want to be really clear about this.

If you buy an FBA Prime-eligible offer and resell it FBA that is technically against Amazon's rules. I do not advocate that. The tactics I've taught have only been for buying merchant-fulfilled, as in non-FBA offers, and selling them FBA. Amazon is very clear about this. There is no policy against what I've described here. Amazon's very, very clear about that. I'm not necessarily saying they love it. I don't know. I just know they don't have a policy about it. Their policy only pertains to using Prime.

Q: "Is the textbook season longer than just August?"

It goes into September. It starts to trail off significantly after the first few days of September. But people are buying textbooks all year round, don't get me wrong. This is not just a seasonal thing. And I should have been more clear about that. Textbooks are not strictly seasonal.

So these are not just tactics to use just before textbook season. That's when the prices spike, but you can do this all year long. There's no reason that you have to limit this activity to just before textbook season.

Q: "How many books per week can you procure this way?"

I personally believe that the opportunity is limitless. I've certainly never...I've run out of money before I've run out of opportunity.

Q: "What percentage of your sales are from online arbitrage?"

That's a great question. Lately it has been upwards of 50%. And it would be a lot more than that if I didn't have such a huge back-catalog, bunch of inventory at FBA. But I'm so hooked on this.

And I have to get in and say this sort of begs the question of, "Well, if this is so good why are you sharing this with other people?" Right? That's exactly what I would be thinking if I was you. So I just want to be clear that I do not believe there's a scarcity of opportunity.

I have less money than there is opportunity. Right? So there's no reason that I can't share this with you guys. It's not going to affect my sourcing options. I've got keywords. I've got stuff that I'm not worried about other people figuring out and I don't have that much money. Or I don't have endless amounts of money.

Q: "Are there condition guidelines for online book arbitrage? Will you buy Acceptable books?"

I will buy Acceptable books. I'm more loose about buying Acceptable books just before textbook season, like right now which is why now is the time, you guys. This is like gold rush time. Seriously. This is legit gold rush time. There is so much opportunity because sales and prices are going to spike so dramatically high in the next couple of weeks, starting in about two weeks. So this is going to blow up.

Q: "Why limit your purchase-ceiling to $10 with all the $250 to $300 books on Amazon?"

That's a great question. You know, because there's so much opportunity I limit my purchases to $10 because I can. That's really it. I mean if you want to go upwards from there and spend $30 or $40 you can flip those for $125 all day long. Absolutely. So yes. As I said before the fields get more fertile for those who are willing...The people who are willing to pay the most.

Q: "Where is Amazon's advanced search option located again?"

It's really easy to miss.

You have to go into a category. You have to go into the books category first and then you'll see it just below the search bar. There's a horizontal line of text and you just click on...You'll see, I think it's like the second one from the left. It'll say Advanced Search.

Q: "How well does this work with other book categories that are not textbooks?"

I've gotten some feedback from other people who do online book arbitrage who say I focus too much on textbooks and that's probably true. So, yeah, there's no reason to limit this to textbooks. Not at all. You can do this with anything as long as you know your numbers.

Q: "A lot of times you get books in worse condition than described. How do you deal with that?"

Every time I've gotten a book in worse condition than described I've gotten a refund. I've never had a seller short me for a refund.

And then you can still sell the book which... Obviously I wouldn't abuse that. But you can still sell it. Because people will still pay a lot more for Acceptable-condition books via FBA. It's not like they won't sell.

So, yeah, I've had that happen to me actually, probably like 10% of the time I'll get a book that didn't mention highlighting that has highlighting, I email the seller, and I get a refund instantly. That's how responsible sellers handle their business. That's how I handle my business.

Q: "Why not buy New offers from merchant-fulfilled sellers?"

Yeah, you can. Absolutely. I didn't mean to emphasize Used. You can absolutely do New books merchant-fulfilled. There's no reason not to.

Q: "Your max price point is $10? Do you buy up all the books from the different sellers under your maximum price point?"

That's a great question. I don't do too many duplicates but there's no reason not to. I hope that makes sense. There's so many options to buy...

There's just so much opportunity I don't feel like I have to buy duplicates. It's not like on a particular day I'm like, "Shoot. I'm out of options. I'm just going to go buy the same book eight times." But you could do that, 100% you could do that.

Q: "Do you buy from 90% sellers with positive feedback?"

So the question basically is, *"If someone has really poor feedback will you still buy from them?"* I don't even really look at that very much because I've never had a problem with people not giving me a refund when I've asked. I've never felt cheated so far. So I don't think that's too much of an issue.

Q: "How much do your sales increase during the textbook season?"

Great question, Tish. My biggest months are August and January. So I would say easily, easily 50%. I don't have those numbers. I don't know those numbers. But 50% is pretty safe. I would say maybe even 200%. I just don't know

Q: "What is the average time that your books sell during non-textbook season?"

You know, Evette, that is an impossible question to answer simply because there are so many variables involved.

I code my SKUs so I can identify what's a textbook, every August I will go back and look at what's leftover from the year before and it's very, very...It's like maybe 15% of the books haven't sold in a year. So the sell-through rate is really, really high despite pricing really, really aggressively.

Q: "Do you buy merchant-fulfilled books through your Amazon seller account? Or do you have a separate buyer account?"

That's a great question. I have not found the need to compartmentalize. I have seen numerous emails from Amazon very unambiguously stating that they do not have a problem with people buying non-Prime-eligible books or anything and reselling it FBA. So there's really no reason to compartmentalize like that.

Q: "When you disregard the first few FBA offers do you check first to see if they are selling multiple copies? If so how many copies for sale is acceptable?"

Yeah. I missed talking about that. That is an awesome question. Thanks, Jim. I should have gotten to that. If you're thinking about pricing higher than the lowest FBA seller and hoping that they'll sell out you want to go ahead and click "add to cart" for their offer and then you increase the quantity to 999 and then hit refresh cart and it will show you the number of copies they have available.

Update: A new browser extension just came out that automates this. It's called "How Many," and tells you exactly how many copies of each book a particular seller has in stock.

So it's usually just going to be one but sometimes with the mega-sellers they'll have like 10 or 15 copies in which case you don't want to try to compete with that. You probably just want to pass on that, or plan on matching their price.

Q: "So how much does a lowest merchant-fulfilled price history play into your pricing if at all?"

It does not factor in at all. But it does factor into what I search for. So I don't like to search for penny books, I'd rather search for $0.02 and up books because the opportunity increases exponentially.

And if you don't understand what I mean by that check out a post I made on FBA Mastery last week called like "The Penny Book Profit Formula" or something like that. And I kind of went into why it is that books priced more than a penny have a much higher likelihood of high-priced FBA offers. It's pretty simple economics.

Q: "So someone says they're looking at a book that has FBA offers of $5.64 in Acceptable condition, $27.26 good, $46 good, and then higher, and has a sales rank of 1.2 million. "I can buy it for $1.65. Would you buy it and what would you sell it for?"

Great question. So, given those stats you gave me if it has a sales rank of 1.2 million I would look at the sales rank history. I'd go on CamelCamelCamel or use the Keepa extension. I would look at the history and I would say, "Okay, in the last three months what's the lowest sales rank it's been?" And I would say if it's hasn't been much lower than 1.2 million I would probably not touch it. In fact 1.2 million would be kind of like my max threshold. Maybe 1.5 for a textbook in the off-season because those can spike. But I really wouldn't touch that. I would make sure that $5.64 offer only has one copy for sale. Use that trick I mentioned where I hit like 99 copies in the quantity field and see how many they actually have for sale.

Q: "Do you ever price FBA Used offers above New?"

That's a great question. You know, I'll tell you when I do and when I don't. I will if the FBA offer is a third-party seller and I will not if it's Amazon itself. The reason is that Amazon itself will always own the Buy Box for new books. And it can happen that people just miss the New portion of the Buy Box. But generally I won't get that bold.

But if it's a third-party seller and say their lowest FBA offer is $20, yeah, I'll price my used offer at $100 because I don't believe most people are going to click over to New and Used and look at both. I think they're just going to look at Used. Whereas if it's in the Buy Box I think they're much more likely to see that.

Q: "Is Add All an extension or a website?"

AddAll is an extension. You go to AddAll.com. They don't advertise it very much, it's only for Firefox, and in the right-hand column you will see an option to add it. But it's very subtle. That's why you're not finding it. I don't think you can find it in the extension store on Firefox?

Q: Terry says, "Keepa extension just stays open as you're looking at the offers. CamelCamelCamel extension won't show you ranked unless you click through to the site. So maybe I'll switch."

That's why I use Keepa. You can see the sales rank history on CamelCamelCamel but you actually have to go to the site.

Q: "Peter, how do you know if a new edition of the textbook has come out?"

It doesn't matter. That's the answer. I don't know or care if a new textbook edition has come out.

It doesn't matter because they might be on the 10th edition for something and I'll still be selling the 5th edition. That's not something I worry about. I would defer entirely to the sales rank history.

Q: "I have sold non-book items above Amazon's price and gotten the sale when Amazon sells out. Have you done this with books?"

I have done that a lot. But you just kind of have to stumble upon those.

But, yes, if Amazon's sold out, I mean I think I posted a story a couple of months ago about how I sold "The American Sniper" book for like $130 because Amazon had sold out.

Q: "Could you comment on using a non-Prime account, using Super Saver Shipping. This seems to be a great big gray area."

I don't think Amazon has a policy about that but I will advise against that because I think if a lot of people started to do it Amazon would develop a policy.

So it's an investment in the long-term. That's a gray area for sure.

Q: "I graded books very conservatively to keep customer satisfaction high. I will list a book at Good when many consider it is Very Good. Am I losing money?"

No. I don't think you are. Not at all. I've actually done some really amateur statistical analysis of this and I do not see a Very Good copy selling at a statistically significantly higher rate than a Good condition book. Now, the sales do drop with Acceptable and I would never list something as Like New except under a couple of very narrow circumstances.

Q: "Would a user have to be a Prime member to take advantage of the Prime-only search function?"

No. You click the "free shipping" option. So if you're logged out of Prime or you don't have Prime at all a box will be there at the top that says "free shipping" and that is synonymous with Prime.

Q: "Will you go over what the Context Search extension does again? I'm having trouble getting it to work."

You highlight an ISBN, you right click, then you scroll down to "AddAll" and you click on AddAll and then it brings up a new window, a new tab and it searches all of these different bookselling sites. Amazon.Japan, Everybody.

I would say 90% of the time the offer that you're seeing on Amazon is going to be the lowest price. However, often times it's not. So it can pay to do that search.

So let's see...Yeah, I'm having fun. I don't ever get to do this, just hang out and talk. So this is really cool. I think if I do this you'll see my face.

Q: "Do you ever sell fiction books?"

Yes, I sell fiction. It's just, I don't care what the book is if it'll make me money.

Q: Kim says, "Textbook ranked 660,000, highest rank in last 3 months is 860,000. No FBA sellers new or used, lowest merchant-fulfilled price is $10. Lowest merchant-fulfilled new price is $33."

I would snatch that up in a second and I would price it at $50.

Q: "Amazon's $172, one's selling for $25."

Okay, I assume that means there's no FBA sellers at all. If you had the money I would buy it. Yeah. I would spent $25, $30 on a book. I don't do it that often but I would if there was literally no other FBA sellers and the sales rank history was strong. Yeah, I would do that and I'd price it at...I'd probably price it $100 and I'm not going to say with certainty that book will sell during textbook season that's coming up but yeah, I would totally do that. And then, you know what? Unless you're totally broke I would do it and then if it doesn't sell then you can always lower the price.

Q: "Do you have any personal criteria for being the second or third lowest price?"

I do. But it's not based in science. It's based on observational data that I have accumulated over the years. If a book is ranked, let's say, 30,000, which means it's probably selling a few copies a day, I'm very comfortable being the third or fourth lowest price, especially right now (i.e. during the textbook sales spike). Right now, things are only gonna go up from here.

Just as an example, a 30,000-ranked book, I'm very comfortable being... Right now third or even fourth, or even fifth, for that matter. I don't think it's too unreasonable to think that three or four or five FBA offers of a book that's selling multiple copies a day are gonna sell out.

Now, it doesn't mean that people can't ship in more copies now, and that you'll still have additional competition, but you can use my guidelines as a starting point, and then you can sort of deviate from there.

Let's say, if you look at a book right now and it's ranked 250,000, that book is maybe only selling one copy a day. You might want to get a little more conservative. You might want to be the lowest price, or second lowest. But even that, I think, is still being overly cautious.

Sales rank is such a fluid thing. But hopefully that gives you a starting point.

Q: "At what sales rank do you price to get the next sale, instead of waiting [by pricing more than $3.99 higher]?"

My rule of thumb is around 1.2 million, I generally start to price $3.99 higher. Meaning, I want that top spot. This is just what I've come to over the years. I don't apply this to textbooks. A textbook that's ranked 1.2 million in December, rather, that book might actually stay pretty well ranked throughout January, and even other times of the year. So I would consider the type of book and look at its sales history.

1.2 million is roughly where I start to go ,"Okay, I kind of want this book to get the top spot. I want to make sure I'm the next sale."

But, with that said, I know people that practice a different formula, a more liberal formula, and they still do well for themselves.

Extras

Sales rank cheat sheet
Profit margin cheat sheet
Interviews
My $1,000 a month profit formula

Sales Rank Cheat Sheet

Here is a quick guide on how to interpret sales rank:

Sales ranks of books selling multiple copies a day:

Sales rank of 1: 10,000 copies per day.
Sales rank 10: 400 copies per day.
Sales rank of 100: 70 copies per day.
Sales rank of 1,000: 30 copies per day.
Sales rank of 5,000: 15 copies a day.
Sales rank of 10,000: 10 copies a day.
Sales rank of 100,000: 1.5 copies a day.

Approximate time since a book last sold:

Sales rank of 300,000: 1 day ago.
Sales rank of 500,000: 3 days ago. (2 to 5 days)
Sales rank of 650,000: 5 days ago. (3 to 7 days)
Sales rank of 800,000 7 days ago. (5 to 9 days ago)
Sales rank of 1,000,000: 10 days ago. (5 to 15 days ago)
Sales rank of 1.2 million: 15 days ago. (8 to 20 days ago)
Sales rank of 1.5 million: 25 days ago. (12 to 35 days ago)
Sales rank of 2.5 million: 40 days ago. (20 to 60 days)

Cheat sheet:
Average selling price to double, triple, & quadruple your money at various purchasing prices

Commission estimates based on average textbook weight of 3.5 pounds. For smaller books, lower sales prices required to meet the stated margins.

Penny books (One cent + $3.99 postage)

Double your money

$14.30 sales price
=$8.03 payout

Triple your money

$19 sales price
= $12.08 payout

Quadruple your money

$23.75 sales price
= $16.07 payout

Dollar books ($1 + $3.99 postage)

Double your money

$16.75 sales price
= $10.12 payout

Triple your money

$22.50 sales price
= $15 payout

Quadruple your money

$28.50 sales price
= $20.10 payout

Two dollar books ($2 + $3.99 postage)

Double your money

$19 sales price
= $12.08 payout

Triple your money

$26.25 sales price
= $18.19 payout

Quadruple your money

$33.25 sales price
= $24.14 payout

Three dollar books ($3 + $3.99 postage)

Double your money

$21.50 sales price
= $14.15 payout

Triple your money

$29.75 sales price
= $21.17 payout

Quadruple your money

$38 sales price
= $28.18 payout

Four dollar books ($4 + $3.99 postage)

Double your money

$23.75 sales price
= $16.07 payout

Triple your money

$33.25 sales price
= $24.14 payout

Quadruple your money

$42.50 sales price
= $32 payout

Five dollar books ($5 + $3.99 postage)

Double your money

$26.25 sales price
= $18.19 payout

Triple your money

$36.75 sales price
 = $27.12 payout

Quadruple your money

$47.25 sales price
= $36.04 payout

Online Book Arbitrage
THE INTERVIEWS

What follows are 4 short interviews with devotees of an emerging practice: People buying cheap books online, and selling them at a higher price via FBA.

Within this framework, there are quite a few models - and I'm learning about more every day.

It seems like every methodology, no matter how crude, is being used with success right now.

Of the people interviewed here, some are newer and have accumulated some cool tricks very quickly. Others, I've been told privately, have some seriously advanced tactics that they aren't willing to divulge fully here, but are still sharing some cool tricks you can get started with.

Check out these interviews to get the gears turning.

-Peter Valley

Sean

How did you get turned on to the idea of buying books on Amazon, and reselling back on Amazon via FBA?

It all started when I found out about Nathan Holmquist from booktothefuture.com. I can't remember exactly how I heard about him. I believe it was on an episode of the Thrifting for Profit podcast by Debra Conrad. After I heard that he sells books on Amazon I decided to learn more. I couldn't believe he makes a full time income selling books on Amazon. It's amazing! I read his blog posts to learn about guidelines he uses to select books.

I was in the dark for a while about Peter Valley, but when I found out about his success and blog I knew I had to read more. Finding more people making a full time income selling books on Amazon encouraged me to keep going. I started spending more money and taking more risks. Additionally, their blogs gave me more knowledge about sourcing and to this day keep me going.

Can you tell us a little about your approach to online book arbitrage? I've heard of several methods. What's yours?

My approach to online book arbitrage is to use eBay to search for books and then go over to Amazon to see if they are profitable and within my sales rank guidelines. I originally tried doing Amazon to Amazon flips but it was very time consuming. For me, using eBay's search filters helped me target books quickly. For example, you can go to the eBay textbook section and limit the price of the books to $5 or less with free shipping. That way you can automatically filter through anything you don't want and only pick the books that meet your criteria.

What's your personal buying formula, in terms of profit margins, sales rank, etc?

Here's my personal online book arbitrage buying formula at this moment:

1. I spend no more than $70 daily and aim to purchase books that equal at least $150 profit. My logic is that if I source books worth $150 profit I will sell 70% of those books in two months or less. This gives me an estimated $100/day ($36k annually). I use this estimation to hedge risk. I will alter this methodology as I collect data and hope to scale it quickly to make more profit.

2.   I target books with a sales rank of <1 million because I want to flip them as fast as possible. When I'm able to pursue this full time I will test longer investments.

What's the biggest mistake you made at first, that others could learn from?

My biggest mistake was not using sales rank as a factor in my purchasing decisions. Now I have books with a 13M sales rank that might not ever leave the warehouse. For beginners I recommend a sales rank of 2M or less (less is always better). That way you can see results quicker and validate the business for yourself. There's nothing better than opening your Amazon Seller app and seeing sales. That in itself should give you the push to go bigger.

What's the best online book arbitrage trick that you're willing to share?

I'll give two tricks because I feel these are both equal in value:

1. If you find a profitable book using specific filter criteria on eBay, copy and paste the URL of that search and put it in a document somewhere. That way when you source again you can just paste the URL into the web browser and it will take you directly to that search. This saves a ton of time and increases the chance that you'll find a profitable book quicker.

2. Analyze your previous orders in Amazon SellerCentral and see if you can buy more of those books you've already sold. This is great because it's already proven that the books will sell. I've done it before and I'll do it again.

Mike Monticue

How did you get turned on to the idea of buying books on Amazon, and reselling back on Amazon via FBA?

I actually heard an NPR podcast about a guy who had software developed for text books. He would buy textbooks during "down" periods when the prices were lower, store them and sell them Merchant Fulfilled during peak seasons at huge markups. I figured if he could do this Merchant-Fulfilled and be profitable – the potential of selling these books on FBA had to be even higher!

Can you tell us a little about your approach to online book arbitrage? I've heard of several methods. What's yours?

Common sense would tell you to search the top-ranked books on Amazon and try to buy these low. Usually though, the very high ranked books are still very expensive – even when sold merchant-fulfilled. Since I don't really know any tricks to finding lists of books ranked in the range I'm looking for – I'll usually double check any textbook that I happen to be listing that fits my criterea and see if there are cheap copies available. I'll also pull a spreadsheet from InventoryLab and go through books I have in inventory or sold in the past and that gives me several hundred books to choose from and search through for lower priced copies.

What's your personal buying formula, in terms of profit margins, sales rank, etc?

Since I'm not buying a large quantity of books – I like to have huge markups – somewhere around 5x my buying price. As far as sales rank - I love to be in the 100K-300K range but I'll go higher if the markup is good. I'm not too concerned with sales rank because I figure if a book is ranked 750K in the offseason, it's going to climb way up during peak seasons.

What's the biggest mistake you made at first, that others could learn from?

I've been taking this slow so I haven't really made any mistakes yet. I also had previous experience flipping other products that I buy online. I would definitely advise to start off slow and develop a system before you pour a ton of cash into it.

Mike has a cool You Tube channel where he shares bookselling tricks. Check it out: https://www.youtube.com/channel/UCdFk7LE47u3WjRGh1hS4Cnw

Michael

How did you get turned on to the idea of buying books on Amazon, and reselling back on Amazon via FBA?

Shortly after I started to get a hang of being a full time bookseller on Amazon, I would notice while pricing my merchant fulfilled items, that some items would be priced way too low. Already having a merchant fulfilled inventory of over 10K titles, I was well aware of this erroneous pricing strategy, and instead, focused my efforts on achieving premium prices for my items rather than quick sells. This would lead me to buying out merchant offers so my higher price could be lower in the search results. I wasnt always making hefty returns on the items I bought, but I wasn't losing money and I was also increasing the sales price of my items. This then evolved into trying to search for these opportunities, and buying textbooks in the off season at very low prices, and then pricing them quite high and slow selling them during textbook season. When we eventually switched to being 100% FBA, we started realizing these inflated margins on 50% or more of our sales.

Often times we were selling $0.01 items for over $35+. I started checking my sales daily (over 100-200 sales a day at this point) and I would look at sales over $20 and check what the merchant price was. If it was profitable I would buy copies. Sometimes lots of copies. Our sales, are still one of the main ways we locate these MFN->FBA flips. Since we price all our inventory only against other FBA offers, they present themselves quite often.

What's your personal buying formula, in terms of profit margins, sales rank, etc?

It really depends. I use CamelCamelCamel and Keepa to see the sales history of an item. I try not to invest too much into items with ranks closer to a million. If im confident that the copies will sell fairly quick (within 6 months), I will buy as many as I think I can sell. I prefer to stay under 250K rank, but I examine each situation individually. I usually dont buy more than 10 copies of a title at a time, however I have purchased as many as 20 from a single seller with poor pricing mechanics.

What's the biggest mistake you made at first, that others could learn from?

When I first started doing this, I didnt know what I know now about rank and how it behaves. I didnt know about CamelCamelCamel or Keepa. On top of that I was scared to invest more than $25 into a book. Dont be scared to invest when you find winners, and know all the tools you have available to you and use them wisely.

What's the best online book arbitrage trick that you're willing to share?

Probably recognizing when youve made a sale that is repeatable and using that to buy more copies, in conjunction with buying out other peoples offers to raise the price of the lowest offer. Also, buying textbooks in the off season for pennies and selling them in JUL-AUG or DEC-JAN. Remember that if you are selling an item FBA it has many advantages over a merchant fulfilled item, so you shouldnt be pricing against merchant offers. They are not your competition. I forget where I read it, but I once read a statement that said something like "90% of Amazon customers have never purchased anything that wasnt fulfilled by Amazon".

Jason

How did you get turned on to the idea of buying books on Amazon, and reselling back on Amazon via FBA?

When I began to notice price discrepancies on books large enough to profit from with a rank low enough that I knew I could sell it. I asked people in a Facebook group and most of them said they wouldn't pay that much for a book but I looked at it not as a book but as a product with an ROI.

Can you tell us a little about your approach to online book arbitrage? I've heard of several methods. What's yours?

Honestly the same way your research went (*Referring to my article: "How I discovered the world's largest book source (Hint: It's Amazon)" -PV*). Mostly hunting and pecking. Sort order helps and so does searching for books that I know have a high enough value.

What's your personal buying formula, in terms of profit margins, sales rank, etc?

For me it's books less than 150,000 when it comes to online arbitrage and I want to make at least a 50% return. This is because I'm looking for a faster return and guaranteed flip.

What's the biggest mistake you made at first, that others could learn from?

None so far that I can recall.

What's the best online book arbitrage trick that you're willing to share?

Some books are worth paying more for. It's a product not a book. There's a mindset that we shouldn't pay much for books but I'll pay $70 for a 50% return on clothing. Why not similar thinking for a book?

You've outsourced a big part of your business. Can you talk about that?

There are many ways to outsource. Im not a fan of listing books as its too time consuming. The thrill of the hunt interests me more so I pay a trusted employee to clean, list, and ship my books. You need an intelligent person because they must accurately grade, describe, and price the book. Most people are against and for good reason - your account is on the line and you must give someone access to your account. I'd rather spend my time looking for more books to buy than cleaning and describing a book. That's why trust is crucial but your company can't grow to its full potential if the owner is the only employee. You'll easily double your profitability if you do this and what many people don't know is that you can give an employee access to the account but limit what they can see using settings found in seller central.

My $1,000 a month profit formula

Here it is: my formula for using my online book arbitrage system to make an extra $1,000 a month (*I can't make any income claims or guarantees here, this is just a theoretical formula that I hope will work for you*):

Target profit: $1,000 a month.
  Average profit per book: $15.
  Conservative prediction: 25% the first month. (It can work out a lot better than this, I just kept the numbers very conservative).

Using this math:
  Target monthly book purchases: 270 a month.
  Target weekly book purchases: 68 books a week.

Your online book arbitrage schedule:
  Average books per hour: Three.
  Average days per week: 5
  Average hours per day: 4.5

So commit to 13 or 14 purchases per day, 5 days a week.

It gets even better:

With these (conservative) figures, after you hit this target profit *you still have 75% of your books left to sell.*

So that $1,000 is just the beginning. After you put $1,000 in your pocket, you'll (hopefully) still have $3,000 headed your way!

All of these numbers are conservative. You will hopefully find more than 3 books per hour, and hopefully profit even more than $15 per book. And your "work" hours will decrease accordingly.

An expanded version of this formula (with two alternate formulas to try out) can be found at: https://zenarbitrage.clickfunnels.com/online-book-arbitrage-book

Sound cool? Email me and let me know how this goes: fbamastery@gmail.com

About the author

Peter Valley is a longtime Amazon seller, whom Bill Nye once told: "Peter, don't ever get a job. It's not worth it."

He is the founder of online book arbitrage tool Zen Arbitrage (ZenArbitrage.com).

CPSIA information can be obtained
at www.ICGtesting.com
Printed in the USA
FSOW03n1525041116
26876FS